God's
power

IS GREATER THAN

willpower

LIFEWAY
GIRLS |
DEVOTIONS

Published by LifeWay Press®

No part of this work may be reproduced or transmitted in any form or by any means, electronic or mechanical, including photocopying and recording, or by any information storage or retrieval system, except as may be expressly permitted in writing by the publisher. Requests for permission should be addressed in writing to LifeWay Press®, One LifeWay Plaza, Nashville, TN 37234.

ISBN 978-1-0877-4259-5
Item 005831568
Dewey Decimal Classification Number: 242
Subject Heading: DEVOTIONAL LITERATURE / BIBLE STUDY AND TEACHING / GOD

Printed in the United States of America

Student Ministry Publishing
LifeWay Resources
One LifeWay Plaza
Nashville, Tennessee 37234

publishing team

Director, Student Ministry
Ben Trueblood

Manager, Student Ministry Publishing
John Paul Basham

Editorial Team Leader
Karen Daniel

Writer
Jesse Campbell

Content Editor
Stephanie Cross

Production Editor
Brooke Hill

Graphic Designer
Kaitlin Redmond

table of contents

intro

It's almost impossible to eat just one chocolate chip cookie (unless you don't like chocolate, which is even rarer than stopping at just one cookie). Or maybe your weakness is buying cute scrunchies or phone covers. Or maybe you're absolutely addicted to seeing what your celebrity crush is up to on social media. While it's okay to have a few cookies, or a couple of cute scrunchies and an adorable phone cover, or even follow your celebrity crush on social media—an over-indulgence of anything isn't healthy. It's not good for your heart, your soul, or your mind. But the truth is that some things just feel really tough to control.

And some of our obsessions are more dangerous than others. While a cute scrunchy is functional and helpful, what about the time you spend comparing yourself to other girls online—wishing you looked more, sounded more, or had more like her? Or maybe you even end up spiraling, clicking link after link until you end up viewing images that you know deep in your heart aren't honoring to you or God. Every single person on this earth, even the girl you think has it all together, struggles with self-control in some area.

While we may not all struggle with the same issues or to the same extent, there is one solution for us all: Jesus. But this isn't just a "church" answer. When you trust in Jesus as Savior, you receive the Holy Spirit. He helps you to remember what God has taught you and do what Scripture commands (Luke 12:12; John 14:26). A major indicator of the Holy Spirit's presence in our life is the fruit of the Spirit—one of which is self-control.

As we walk through this devotional over the next 30 days, we'll study Scripture that teaches why self-control is important, what role it plays in revealing our identity, how Satan tempts us, what to do when we feel tempted, and how to live godly, self-controlled lives.

These devos will challenge you. They will push you to examine your life, examine your heart, and lean heavily on the Holy Spirit's presence in your life. When you feel discouraged, remember that He is with you every step of the way. Remember that God's power is so much greater than our willpower. And no matter how many times you fail, God's grace waits on the other side.

getting started

This devotional contains 30 days of content, divided into sections that answer a specific question about self-control. Each day is broken down into three elements—discover, delight, and display—to help you answer core questions related to Scripture.

discover

This section helps you examine the passage in light of who God is and determine what it says about your identity in relationship to Him. Included here is the key passage and focus Scripture, along with illustrations and commentary to guide you as you study.

delight

In this section, you'll be challenged by questions and activities that help you see how God is alive and active in every detail of His Word and your life. You'll be guided to ask yourself about what the passage means for your relationship with God.

display

Here's where you really take action. Display calls you to apply what you've learned through each day's study.

prayer

Each day also includes a prayer activity in one of the three main sections.

Throughout the devotional, you'll also find extra articles and activities to help you connect with the topic personally, such as Scripture memory verses, additional resources, and questions.

day 1

BOUGHT

discover|

READ 1 CORINTHIANS 6:19-20.

Don't you know that your body is a temple of the Holy Spirit who is in you, whom you have from God? You are not your own, for you were bought at a price. So glorify God with your body.

Imagine your parents give you a beautiful diamond promise ring. Its price tag reads $3,000. They paid full price for it and entrusted it to you. It's the only one they will ever give you. How would you care for this ring? Would you let dirt and grime build up around the stones, or would you keep it safe in the velvet box far away from any possibility of being scratched, lost, or damaged?

The Corinthians, the recipients of Paul's letter, thought the temple in Jerusalem was where God's direct presence dwelled. While it might sound a little weird to us—our bodies being temples—Paul was helping the Corinthians (and us) grasp that the Holy Spirit dwells within believers when they trust in Jesus for salvation. This is why Paul called their bodies a temple of the Holy Spirit.

You are way more valuable than a new promise ring. Your purchase price was much greater than $3,000—it was God's only Son, Jesus. This is what Paul meant when He said you are not your own; you belong to God. Now the Holy Spirit lives in you, making you a temple. The presence of the Holy Spirit fundamentally changes you. The very Spirit of God lives within you and His presence in your life produces fruit: one part of that fruit is self-control.

delight |

When have you tried to live a self-controlled life in your own strength? What happened?

How does it comfort you to know that the Holy Spirit is the One who empowers us to live self-controlled lives and that He dwells within us?

display |

How incredible is it that all people are made in the image of God? Our bodies already have such incredible value, but when we are filled with the Holy Spirit and grasp the price Jesus paid on the cross to redeem us, we get a better idea of just how valuable we are to God. We represent more than ourselves—we represent Him.

Use pages 16-17 to memorize 1 Corinthians 6:19-20. Meditate on this passage, listening carefully to the Holy Spirit's conviction for ways you might not be glorifying God with your body. Always remember you are His, and do whatever is necessary to turn away from sin—even if it seems extreme. When we do this, we show love and respect to our Father, treasuring His priceless gift.

Listen to the song "Who You Say I Am" by Hillsong Worship. Allow the lyrics to remind you that you belong to the God of all and He loves you deeply.

> Confess to God ways you have failed to glorify Him with your body. Thank Him for His forgiveness and for His presence within you. Ask Him to help you practice self-control and commit your body to His glory.

day 2

MINDSET

discover|

Ask God to direct your mind, focusing it on Him. Confess if you have been entangled in the things of this world like materialism or popularity and acceptance from those who do not know Him.

READ ROMANS 8:5-6.

For those who live according to the flesh have their minds set on the things of the flesh, but those who live according to the Spirit have their minds set on the things of the Spirit. Now the mindset of the flesh is death, but the mindset of the Spirit is life and peace.

The more you think about something, the more consuming it becomes. Repeated thoughts become thought-patterns (go-to ways of thinking), which form our mindset (our mental attitude). These direct our focus for better or worse. It can be so easy to allow our mindset to become focused on the world around us rather than the Spirit within us.

Paul said "the mindset of the Spirit is life and peace" (v. 6). That sounds amazing, right? In the Spirit you find peace that things of this world can never bring. Ultimately, sin brings death—which is exactly what we deserve when we devote our lives to serving the flesh. But God's priceless gift to us through Jesus is eternal life and peace (Rom. 6:23).

delight |

This passage is more than a call to stop doing sinful things; it's a call to completely redirect our focus. How does it tell us to do that?

In what way does it benefit us to set our minds on the Spirit?

display |

We move toward what we focus on, so if we focus on the things of this world, we'll follow a path of sin. However, if we focus on the things of God, we'll be following a path of righteousness.

Keep a journal with you over the next 24-hours. Jot down any thoughts you notice popping up often. At the end of the day, review your list. How many of the thoughts would be considered part of the "mindset of the flesh"? How many thoughts would be considered part of the "mindset of the Spirit"? Overall, where did your focus lie—on things of the flesh or the Spirit?

What are some practical ways you can train yourself to set your mind on the Spirit? Write out any Scripture references that guide your answers.

day 3

NO SUPERHEROES

discover |

READ ROMANS 7:18-25.

For I know that nothing good lives in me, that is, in my flesh. For the desire to do what is good is with me, but there is no ability to do it. — Romans 7:18

There are no spiritual superheroes—even our favorite worship leaders and pastors are tempted. Jesus Himself faced the same kinds of temptation we face but was without sin (Heb. 4:15-16). The truth is: No one is exempt. The struggle we experience between Spirit enabled self-control and our sin nature is the same struggle every Christian has faced throughout history. So, take heart, you are not alone. And there is beauty in the struggle—honor in the fact that we fight against sin rather than just give in and feel no conviction.

As Paul made clear in today's Scripture, we can't do any good on our own. It's only by the indwelling of the Holy Spirit (the Holy Spirit living within us) that we have the ability to control ourselves. We can take no credit for the transformation that occurred in us the day we were saved or for the glorification awaiting us when we arrive in heaven. Here and now, as we wait on the future glorification, we experience something called sanctification, a process where the Spirit continually makes us more like Christ and less like our former, sinful selves. We will continue to struggle—and continue to be sanctified—until the end of our life.

delight |

In this chapter, Paul described the struggle between his mind's desire to obey God and his flesh's constant leaning toward sin. How have you experienced this struggle in your own life?

If we had the ability to just do enough good works to save ourselves, would the cross have been necessary? Why not?

display |

Imitate Paul's honest humility in Romans 7 and speak with God about how your flesh just wants to sin. Then, just as Jesus demonstrated in the Lord's Prayer (Matt. 6:9-13), ask God to not bring you to temptation, but to deliver you from the evil one. Pray for the Holy Spirit's presence within you to give you self-control over the flesh.

Just like Paul explained in Romans 7, the constant struggle with our sin nature causes us to understand our need for a Savior. If you have not yet come to terms with your own sin nature, talk with your parents or guardians, pastor, youth pastor or small group leader about what that means. If you have, ask God to continue to grow your faith and help you to lean on the Holy Spirit's leading always.

List three good things God has done through you recently. Then, write over the list in large letters, *God gets the credit* as a reminder that all of the good we do points back to and glorifies God.

day 4

BROKEN-DOWN WALL

discover|

READ PROVERBS 25:28.

A person who does not control his temper is like a city whose wall is broken down.

Imagine your favorite princess story or movie. Now, think about the castle—specifically the walls. You're probably envisioning something grand and tall with gates that can be lowered to allow entry. Maybe there's even a moat with frightening creatures to keep the bad guys away. Although these stories are make-believe, the castles had walls to protect much like the cities in the Bible.

In the ancient world, a city's defense was a wall. Without a wall to protect them from intruders, a city was vulnerable to attack. Just like these walls protected the princesses and the ancient world, we have to defend ourselves from attack, too—and one way we defend ourselves is with self-control. When we lose our temper, we are as vulnerable to attack as an ancient city without a wall.

There is a difference between being angry and sinning. In fact, the apostle Paul wrote, "Be angry and do not sin" (Eph. 4:26), which reveals that feeling emotions of anger is not wrong. Going off on someone and losing our cool is wrong, though. One of the ways to maintain our walls of defense against attacks from the enemy, is to practice self-control when we are tempted to lose our temper.

delight |

Why is it important to have control over your temper?

In what ways does an uncontrolled temper cause us to be vulnerable to the enemy's attacks?

How can you feel anger, yet refuse to lose control? Who can help you with this?

display |

Think about your relationships. Are there any you have damaged due to a lack of self-control when it comes to your temper? Invite the Holy Spirit to rebuild this broken-down wall in your life. He loves you in your broken state, and He wants your voice to be taken seriously when you speak the gospel. So, for His sake, invite the Holy Spirit to take over your temper both in-person and online. Seek to mend any broken relationships.

List some healthy ways to express anger. Pour your energy and frustration into something that makes you better. These healthy expressions could be artistic, athletic, or worshipful.

Start your prayer by glorifying God. Then, ask Him to heal your heart from past conflicts where you lost your temper. Ask the Holy Spirit to give you self-control, especially in the midst of conflict.

day 5

discover |

READ ROMANS 12:1-2.

Therefore, brothers and sisters, in view of the mercies of God, I urge you to present your bodies as a living sacrifice, holy and pleasing to God; this is your true worship. Do not be conformed to this age, but be transformed by the renewing of your mind, so that you may discern what is the good, pleasing, and perfect will of God.

Have you ever stepped out onto the stage and felt alone? You've finished the final rehearsal with all the last-minute tips from your teacher. Now, it's just you. Your teacher helped you prepare, but now it's time for you to give all that you have to the competition— to leave it all on the stage.

Romans 1-11 contains some of the deepest theology ever written. Then, chapter 12 begins with "Therefore." This means, in light of all that deep theology, here's what you need to do. What Paul was saying in these verses was essentially: "You've received God's mercy, now live it out—with all you are, glorify God." Give your all to Him because He gave everything for you.

We are to present our bodies "as a living sacrifice," which means we won't be like everyone else. Instead, we'll allow God to transform us into new people, to renew our minds. When we do this, we'll engage in true worship that leads us to discern God's will.

delight |

Why would God's mercy cause us to worship?

How does becoming a living sacrifice lead us to self-control?

display |

Self-sacrifice, which leads to self-control, is a foreign concept in our culture. Living your life in pursuit of God's perfect will sets you apart, so you have to get comfortable with feeling out of place.

Worship helps you test and discern God's will for your life because it focuses your heart on Him and not on yourself. In that state, you can see His truth. Gossip, clothes, social media, popularity, and cultural acceptance fade away. Write out the things that have shifted your focus away from God. Now, beside each one, write out a reason you have to worship Him instead.

Take a minute to worship today. Close your eyes, kneel, lift your hands, pray, sing, journal, sit quietly in His presence—do whatever you feel led to do to express your desire to worship God. Jot down one insight He gave you during this time of worship.

Sacrifice your plans, worldly desires, and ambitions on the altar of worship. Ask God to transform you with a renewed mind so you can see the world through His eyes.

"Don't you know that your body is a temple of the Holy Spirit who is in you, whom you have from God? You are not your own, for you were bought at a price. So glorify God with your body."

1 CORINTHIANS 6:19-20

day 6

YOUR HOLY CALLING

discover|

Ask the Holy Spirit to convict you of any unholy conduct.
Be specific when you do. Ask Him to teach you how to be
self-controlled as you pursue holiness.

READ 1 PETER 1:14-16.

As obedient children, do not be conformed to the desires of your former ignorance.
But as the one who called you is holy, you also are to be holy in all your conduct;
for it is written, Be holy, because I am holy.

It takes boldness to tell others, "Be like me." However, when that
boldness is matched with perfection, there is no room to argue. To
be holy is to be set apart, different, and above the things of this
world. God alone is perfect in His holiness and He has called you
to be like Him.

This might seem impossible, but believers are His children—and
He sent His Holy Spirit to help His children be like Him. It is our
calling as Christians to obey God and not live in the ignorance of
our former selves. The word "ignorance" is not an insult (v. 14); it's
simply a lack of knowledge. When we know Him, we can trust Him
and seek to obey His call to holiness in our conduct. This means we
consistently seek to exercise self-control in all areas of life.

---

delight |

What are some reasons it's challenging to "be holy in all [our] conduct" (v. 16)?

Why is holiness incompatible with total acceptance from the world?

display |

In the column labeled, *Temptations*, list any behaviors you're tempted to participate in that do not lead to holiness. Then, in the *Resistance* column, jot down an alternate activity that would help you avoid or resist the temptation. The main question you want to ask yourself as you create this list is: *How can I choose holiness over sin?*

Temptations	Resistance

Review the list and prayerfully consider the way you're tempted most often. Write out on a sticky note, "When I am tempted to _____, I will _____," filling in your resistant behavior in the second blank. Place this on your light switch so you see it when you leave every morning.

day 7

SET FREE

discover

Ask God to remind you of the freedom He has granted you in Jesus. Focus on the truth that Jesus died for you, so that you could be set free from sin and death.

READ 2 PETER 1:3-11.

His divine power has given us everything required for life and godliness through the knowledge of him who called us by his own glory and goodness. By these he has given us very great and precious promises, so that through them you may share in the divine nature, escaping the corruption that is in the world because of evil desire. — 2 Peter 1:3-4

Imagine the feeling you get when the bell rings at the end of the last day before Spring break—you're so ready to escape the four walls of your classroom. As you walk through the halls toward the exit, you begin to feel the excitement of being free. Christ followers have been set free from sin and fully equipped for what is next. The gospel is all for God's own glory, but it includes a glorious promise of freedom from sin for us.

Notice how Peter drew a line from faith to self-control (vv. 5-6). By Jesus' power, we are fully equipped to live godly lives. We have no excuses. We are no longer trapped by our sin nature or the corruption of the world, but have been set free!

delight |

How can godly self-control reduce our temptation toward evil desires and sin? What effect might this have on corruption in the rest of the world?

List some of the "great and precious promises" Paul referenced (v. 4).

display |

The promise of the gospel is salvation for sinners and glory for God, whose divine power makes it possible. Through the power of the Holy Spirit who lives in you, live like you've been set free from your sin—escaping the lie that you have no choice but to sin—and accept the calling to freedom Christ offers.

Sometimes we continue to walk in sin because it's familiar to us, and what's familiar seems easier. Jesus warned us that following Him wouldn't be easy, but He also promised hope for a better future than we can begin to imagine! In a journal, free write about the familiar, sinful habits you're tempted to run back to most often. Explore what makes those so tempting, and as you write, talk openly with God about your struggle. Ask Him to strengthen you to walk in holiness.

God's divine power has given you everything you need for life and godliness. You have been set free. As you consider the specific things God has freed you from, think about how you might share the gospel through your personal testimony. Consider recording a video of your story and sharing with a close friend.

day 8

RUN!

discover |

> Thank God for revealing to you the truth of His gospel message, and ask Him for boldness to share with others what He has done for you. Pray that He would prepare the hearts of the people He has planned for you to share with.

READ 1 THESSALONIANS 5:5-10.

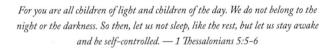

For you are all children of light and children of the day. We do not belong to the night or the darkness. So then, let us not sleep, like the rest, but let us stay awake and be self-controlled. — *1 Thessalonians 5:5-6*

Have you ever seen a suspense or horror movie and wondered about the wisdom of the decisions people make? Do you hide your face behind a pillow, all while calling out to the main character to run for her life (or at least turn on a light!), even as she searches the darkened house all alone? When we see danger, our natural response is to want to warn those who are running straight for it.

Even if all of your friends who do not yet know Jesus are running full-speed into sin, you have the Holy Spirit and are called to self-control. In verse 8, Paul makes it clear that we can't go back to sleep spiritually. Even if we want to join the sinful activities our friends may participate in, we are still called to be children of light. Beyond that, we are also called to warn others of the dangers of sin, calling them to walk in the light alongside us.

delight |

Christians are called to be different from the surrounding culture. How does Paul's use of the words *day* and *night* emphasize this truth? Explain.

What do you think it means to "belong" to the night?

Review Paul's instruction to "stay awake" throughout today's passage. What might staying awake have to do with self-control?

display |

You can't go back to sleep spiritually. You can't unlearn the truth about sin and temptation and the spiritual significance of self-control.

Focus your heart on the Spirit and identify ways you have lacked self-control in the past. Instead of slamming yourself for failing, aspire to holiness in new ways, as a child of the light. Write out five ways you can pursue self-control in those areas instead.

Use a concordance or online search to find all the references to "children of light" in the New Testament. In a journal, write out how these verses increased your understanding of what it means to be a child of the light.

day 9

GRACE INSTEAD

discover |

READ TITUS 2:11-12.

For the grace of God has appeared, bringing salvation for all people, instructing us to deny godlessness and worldly lusts and to live in a sensible, righteous, and godly way in the present age.

Grace changes everything. Grace is loving treatment that we don't deserve. If we were so righteous on our own that God had no choice but to treat us fairly and give us heaven, then there would be no grace involved (Rom. 11:6). It would just be a fair transaction of moral virtue. In reality, we were born depraved and sinful, but Jesus died for us—even while we were still sinners (Rom. 5:8)! What we deserved for our sin was hell, but we received grace instead.

Repenting from sin is the appropriate response to the grace God has so kindly given to us. When we accept the gift of His grace, it is beyond fair for God to instruct us to deny godlessness and worldly lusts (v. 12). Even if our friends who do not yet know Jesus continue in sin, we are called to be holy and to live sensible, righteous, and godly lives (v. 12).

When we truly live as recipients of His amazing grace, the people around us will see a difference. The entire world searches for hope and peace—and our living out of His grace points to the answer, giving us the opportunity to share the reason for our hope and different way of living (1 Pet. 3:15).

delight |

Is it possible for someone to be a Christian without repenting from her sin? Why or why not?

While Jesus' sacrifice was sufficient to bring salvation for all people (v. 11), how does Scripture distinguish those who are saved from those who are not (v. 12)?

display |

As you grow in Christ, you will begin to understand symptoms of belief versus unbelief. Do not look down on your friends who don't know Jesus, but see the reflection of your former self in them. If not for God's grace, you would be doing exactly the same things. Instead, you know how to live a sensible, self-controlled, and godly life.

Read Galatians 5:19-21. How do these verses help you understand what Paul meant by "godlessness and worldly lusts" (v. 12)? Jot down any items from the list you struggle with.

Now, read Galatians 5:22-23. How do these verses help you understand the way the Holy Spirit helps you live a godly life? What fruit do you want to see more of in your life? Ask the Holy Spirit to help you live God's way.

> Pray as Jesus instructed and ask the Father to deliver you from evil (Matt. 6:9-13). Ask Him to deliver you from temptation, and when possible, remove the temptation from your life. God has given you grace, so commit to live in a godly way today (v. 12).

day 10

IT'S GOOD TO STAND OUT!

discover |

> Thank Jesus for the way He defied the crowd with His teaching and even with His silence before angry mobs of mockers. Commit to Him your own willingness to defy the crowd. Pray for His perfect will to be done in everything.

READ 2 TIMOTHY 3:1-5.

But know this: Hard times will come in the last days. —2 Timothy 3:1

Do you have that one friend who is not afraid to put herself out there and do something bold? Maybe you're that girl in your group of friends. The world needs brave souls who are willing to step out first—it's good to stand out! Faith in Christ already makes Christians stand out from the crowd—but Paul goes so far as to tell Timothy to avoid people who dwell in ungodliness.

The "last days" are the days of human history between the first and the second coming of Christ. We are in the last days now, and this passage clearly warns us that they will be difficult—just like Jesus did in John 16:33. These words were written almost 2,000 years ago, but they sound like a blog post written about culture today. Notice that verse 3 even mentions people who will live "without self-control." Practicing self-control will cause us to miss out on some of the fun things our friends will do (v. 4), but our joy—true and lasting—rests in heaven. And because of Jesus, our joy and the good promises of God will never end!

delight |

How have you seen the behaviors listed in verses 2-4 lived out around you?

What does it look like for someone to hold on to a form of godliness, but deny God's power in their lives (v. 5)?

display |

The gospel changes us, and when we live out of that change, we will stand out! Instead of blending in with a world that doesn't have your best interests at heart, own the fact that you will stand out.

Imagine it's February 2026. Where do you want to be in five years? On a blank sheet of notebook paper, write to your best friend from the future. Describe what your life is like now. As you write, make sure to touch on how your life was affected—both negatively and positively—since you stood out because of your faith.

List four ways you can courageously step out in faith and lead in a way that is opposite of the descriptions listed in 2 Timothy 3:1-5. (Hint: Read Colossians 3:12-13.)

How the Holy Spirit Helps When We're Tempted

Throughout Scripture, we see the many roles of the Holy Spirit:

- He helps, reminds and instructs (John 14:26).
- He intercedes for us when we don't know what to pray (Rom. 8:26).
- He produces godly character in our lives (Gal. 5:22-23).
- His presence in our lives marks us as part of God's kingdom (1 Cor. 6:19).
- He is the Helper, the Spirit of truth, and dwells within us (John 14:15-17).
- He brings wisdom and understanding, wise counsel, strength, knowledge and fear of the Lord (Isa. 11:2).
- He empowers us to share the gospel (Acts 1:8).
- He guides us in truth and speaks about the things that will come (John 16:12-15).
- He brings freedom to God's children (2 Cor. 3:17).
- He empowers us to hope, no matter what (Rom. 15:13).
- He convicts of sin (John 16:7-8).
- He helps us to live in obedience to God (Ezek. 36:26-27).
- He teaches us spiritual truths (1 Cor. 2:13).
- He seals us for eternity (Eph. 1:13).

There are certainly more truths concerning the Holy Spirit, but the point is: The Holy Spirit marks us as God's own and empowers us to live life His way. We absolutely cannot overcome temptation without Him. This is one of the reasons Scripture calls Him the Helper: He helps us to understand God's Word and obey it. Part of obeying is avoiding sin. Now, this doesn't mean we will live perfectly for the rest of our lives, but that by listening to the Spirit's guidance, we can say no to the things that tempt us.

While the temptations you experience may be different from the temptations your best friend struggles to overcome, "there is nothing new under the sun" (Eccl. 1:9). In other words, while you may be tempted in different ways than our brothers and sisters in Christ throughout history, the underlying temptations are the same. For example, if you struggle with wanting more followers on social media or obsess over gaining popularity as an influencer, the underlying struggle may be greed, selfishness, insecurity, or arrogance. There are biblical examples of people struggling with this, too. Think about how Martha wanted to be recognized for how hard she worked and served (Luke 10). While it wasn't sinful for her to work hard and serve, her attitude revealed a selfish desire to be noticed.

The Bible gives us timeless wisdom—its commands neither age nor become irrelevant. We can learn, even from narrative stories like that of Martha, how to grow in our relationship with Jesus. But the key thing we need to realize is that, just like Martha, we can't serve God and love others well on our own—we need the presence of Jesus in our lives. We need the Holy Spirit.

Scripture proclaims that "No temptation has come upon you except what is common to humanity. But God is faithful; he will not allow you to be tempted beyond what you are able, but with the temptation he will also provide the way out so that you may be able to bear it" (1 Cor. 10:13). Much like the verse in Ecclesiastes, this verse points out that temptation isn't a new thing. Our being tempted never surprises God—and as He is the God of the universe, it also shouldn't surprise us that He had a plan from the beginning, even for this. But we have to be careful in reading this verse not to think that it says we won't experience temptation. In fact, it declares the opposite: We absolutely will be tempted. However, God will "provide the way out" so that we can withstand the temptation. It's also important to recognize that "what we are able" means "what we can withstand with the power of the Holy Spirit." We can't do this on our own; it is the Holy Spirit who empowers us to live out the Christian life and escape temptation.

When we follow the Spirit's leading, we can face whatever comes our way with "love, joy, peace, patience, kindness, goodness, faithfulness, gentleness, and self-control" (Gal. 5:22-23). But this is something, just like following Jesus, that we have to choose. We have to daily choose to set aside our desires in favor of God's. We can't be self-controlled unless we are Spirit-controlled. As we embrace the Christian life and the role of the Holy Spirit in that life, we can say no to what tempts us and fully embrace the beauty of following God wherever He leads and in whatever He leads us to do.

day 11

BEWARE!

discover |

> Invite the Holy Spirit to examine your heart for areas where you've been weak. As He does, it will likely illuminate something difficult to give up. Remember that holiness is worth any sacrifice. These convictions are also unique to you, and others who do not follow Christ aren't held to them. Ask Him to guard your heart and speech from looking or talking down to others who do not live like you.

READ 1 PETER 5:8.

Be sober-minded, be alert. Your adversary the devil is prowling around like a roaring lion, looking for anyone he can devour.

The thought of being hunted by a lion is unsettling! Have you ever seen signs that read "Beware of Dog"? Usually, this means the dog is aggressive or dangerous, so owners post warnings to visitors. Passages like today's text may not be popular, but they are in God's Word for a reason. God desires to warn us of the dangers of our enemy; this passage screams: "Beware of the enemy!"

If we only had the uplifting verses, then we would be unprepared for the reality of life as Christ followers. So, we must take to heart Peter's instruction to be sober-minded. Simply put: We have to be completely aware of the devil's goals and plans. We must remain alert, watchful, and always beware of the direction of our lives.

delight |

What does the word "prowling" indicate about Satan's approach?

Where have you seen evidence of the enemy "prowling" in your life recently?

display |

One of the biggest lies that Satan tells people is that he is not real and God is to blame for the terrible things that happen every day. Yes, God is in ultimate control, but Satan is responsible for every bad thing that has ever happened. His time of reckoning has been prophesied and set, but it's not yet here. Until then, we must remain watchful, sober-minded, and alert to the powers of evil at work in our world.

Being self-controlled requires us to be self-aware, meaning we have to know ourselves and our personal areas of struggle. But we also have to be aware of the surrounding culture: the messages that come through movies, music, social media, conversations with friends, podcasts, and videos.

- Consider the content you've consumed over the last week. Write out the titles, accounts, and people who've caused (or encouraged you) to act in ungodly ways this week. If it's media of some kind—draw a big, red X over the top of it, signifying that you will remove this from your life (Matt. 5:27-30).

- If people have encouraged you to act in ungodly ways, write out their names and pray for them. Prayerfully consider how much time you spend with those people. While it's good to have friends who believe differently from you—we are called to share the gospel with all people, after all—the people you spend the most time with have the greatest influence on you. Be careful to choose your closest friends wisely.

day 12

SUBMISSION

discover

READ JAMES 4:4-10.

Therefore, submit to God. Resist the devil, and he will flee from you.
— James 4:7

The word *submission* often carries a negative connotation. It implies giving up unwillingly. But when we submit to God, we aren't actually giving up—we're giving ourselves over to Him. In His hands is the only place we will ever find complete protection.

When you submit to God, He towers over you, and the evil one pursuing you has to flee. Verse 6 quotes Proverbs 3:34, revealing God gives grace to the humble. It requires humility to submit to God, but the benefit of having your enemy—the devil—flee from you is totally worth it.

When we refuse to resist the devil, we basically submit to him; it's impossible to submit to both God and the devil. God is omnipresent; the devil isn't. God goes with you wherever you go, but the devil doesn't. The devil is given a degree of freedom for now (Rev. 20:7-10), but even then, he can only tempt you to the extent that God allows (Job 1:6-12). It's a promise that Satan will flee if you resist him.

> **Express to God verbally that you are submitting to Him.**
> **Ask Him to help you sense and resist the enemy's attacks.**

delight |

Why is it important to recognize that we have to submit to God and resist the enemy, but God is the One who causes the enemy to flee?

Reflect on a time when you submitted to God and resisted the devil. What was that experience like?

display |

In the age of feminism, many girls are taught a negative view of the word *submission*, so it's important to understand that submitting to God actually gives us freedom—He loves us sacrificially and we submit willingly to His authority. Write out everything you've heard or believed about submission. Over your list, use green marker to write the words: *Submitting to God means I'm loved, protected, and free.*

day 13

DON'T THINK ABOUT PIZZA

discover |

> Ask the Holy Spirit to bring Scripture to your mind and show you how to apply it in steps throughout the day. Thank God for being the Wonderful Counselor who never leaves us.

READ GALATIANS 5:16.

I say, then, walk by the Spirit and you will certainly not carry out the desire of the flesh.

Whatever you do right now, do not think about pizza. Absolutely do not imagine the strings the cheese makes when you lift a hot slice out of the box. Don't think about a steamy garlic parmesan crust or the buttery crunch it makes when you bite into it. Whatever you do, don't think about the savory toppings. Now, what are you thinking about? Pizza, of course. That is how it goes when you think constantly about not sinning.

Walking by the Spirit is about more than just abstaining from sin: it's about doing God's will. Living a holy lifestyle is not a negative action like simply refusing to do something. It's a positive and deliberate series of actions toward God, taken in obedience by the Spirit's prompting. When you focus only on the next step the Spirit has for you, there is no room for the desire of the flesh. So, Paul's using the word "certainly" in this verse is not an overstatement. When you focus entirely on one thing you forget the other. For example, you have already forgotten about pizza...until now.

delight |

Even though you are a believer, you are still vulnerable to temptation from Satan. How does focusing on the Spirit's presence and leading in your life help you overcome temptation?

Why do you think this verse uses the word "walk"—an active description—by the Spirit?

display |

If you have been focusing on what not to do, it is time to turn your view of self-control upside down. Realign your focus and the rest will follow. If you focus on your temptation, only it will be constantly on your mind. If you focus on the Spirit of God and what you are learning from God's Word, self-control will come more easily. The Spirit's voice will become easier to recognize. The Holy Spirit will speak through His Word and show you the next step of obedience.

Listen today as the Spirit reminds you of Scripture. Each time you are reminded of a verse from the Bible, write it down or leave a voice note on your phone. At the end of the day review all those remembrances. Then, celebrate His work in your life.

Write out a short phrase to help you remember to focus on the Spirit, especially when you feel like you're spiraling out of control.

day 14

RULE OVER IT!

discover|

READ GENESIS 4:3-8.

Then the LORD said to Cain, "Why are you furious? And why do you look despondent? If you do what is right, won't you be accepted? But if you do not do what is right, sin is crouching at the door. Its desire is for you, but you must rule over it." Cain said to his brother Abel, "Let's go out to the field." And while they were in the field, Cain attacked his brother Abel and killed him.
— Genesis 4:6-8

Scripture doesn't say exactly what God expected from Cain and Abel's sacrifices, but Cain knew the expectation (v. 7) and didn't meet it. Abel was keeper of the flocks, and Cain worked in the fields. Abel brought the biggest and best offering he could, while Cain's offering of produce from the fields was not even what God requested. On top of that, he gave the offering with evil in his heart (1 John 3:12). God accepted Abel's offering, but not Cain's. This led to resentment, which led to sin, which ultimately led to Cain committing the first murder.

The truth is: the whole point of sin is our destruction. Satan wants to rule over us, and he does that through sin. If we are casual about sin—as Cain was about his offering—then it will master us. As it masters us, our lives will spiral out of control.

Thankfully, Jesus gave Himself as the ultimate sacrifice for our sins. As we continually walk with Him in trust and obedience, He will help us master sin, which leads to life.

delight |

How does Scripture make it clear that Cain planned to murder his brother (v. 8)?

Do you ever go somewhere or do something, knowing it will probably lead you to sin? How can you choose to walk away from sin instead?

display |

The prophesied day is approaching: Satan will be forever destroyed. Until then, sin still crouches at the door, and you, like Cain, are still called to rule over it (v. 7). You are called to self-control.

Using a dry-erase marker, write out 1 Corinthians 10:13 on your mirror. God provides a way of escape when we're tempted. Look at this before you start each day as a reminder that, through the Holy Spirit, you have the power to say no to temptation and sin.

One of the best ways to rule over sin is to have active accountability in your life. Find another girl who will hold you accountable if you haven't already. This is a girl you can be honest with, even though you will be tempted to lie to her. If you already have an accountability partner in your life, get in touch with her, and let her know that you appreciate the role she plays in your life to help you rule over sin.

Share with God your respect for His warning to Cain that sin crouches at the door. Ask Him to help you rule over sin. Ask Him to lead you away from temptation. Pray for self-control.

day 15

IN CONTEXT

discover|

READ MATTHEW 4:1-11.

> *Again, the devil took him to a very high mountain and showed him all the*
> *kingdoms of the world and their splendor. And he said to him, "I will give you*
> *all these things if you will fall down and worship me." Then Jesus told him, "Go*
> *away, Satan! For it is written: Worship the Lord your God, and serve only him."*
> *Then the devil left him, and angels came and began to serve him.*
> *— Matthew 4:8-11*

There's a scene in *The Lion King* where Mufasa brings Simba to the top of the mountain and shows him the entire kingdom. He told him that everything the light touched belonged to them. Satan did the same thing to Jesus in these verses. One thing the enemy failed to remember is that he can't give away what he doesn't own.

This passage is often taught to show how Jesus used Scripture to fight temptation. But we sometimes overlook the fact that Satan actually quoted the Bible to tempt Jesus. The critical difference between the way Satan used the Bible and Jesus used the Bible is that Jesus used Scripture in context. In fact, if Satan had kept reading the Scripture he quoted to try to tempt Jesus (Ps. 91:11), he would have read verse 13, which explains that the Messiah will trample the serpent. It's important to know the context of a passage before you quote it.

> Ask God for spiritual protection. Ask Him to rebuke Satan and to deliver you from evil, casting away forces of spiritual darkness from you and your family.

delight |

James said, "Therefore, submit to God. Resist the devil, and he will flee from you" (4:7). How did Jesus practice this when the devil tempted Him?

Satan's original sin was pride and the desire to be like the Most High. Where is that motive present in this text?

display |

When you focus on a passage of Scripture, read the whole passage. To interpret the Bible properly, you need to know context. Jesus—being the Word in flesh Himself (John 1:1)—knew how the Bible verses He used fit in the larger picture of redemption and was able to use Scripture properly as a weapon against the enemy. The devil, meanwhile, deliberately removed context from the verses he used to attack the Word Himself.

Satan couldn't give Jesus all the kingdoms of the world because he didn't own them (Ps. 24:1). Satan doesn't own you either—God does. On an index card, write the words *I am His*. Keep it in your pocket, purse, or on your nightstand so you will be constantly reminded of this truth.

Satan might promise you "all of these things" if you focus on him and live like the rest of the world rather than living for God. But every good and perfect gift comes from God (Jas. 1:17). Take a minute to write out all the things (including friendships, new opportunities, and challenges) God has given to you this year. Spend some time thanking Him for each one.

I have
treasured your
word in my
heart so that I
may not sin
against you.

PSALM 119:11

day 16

THE WAY OUT

discover |

READ 1 CORINTHIANS 10:13.

No temptation has come upon you except what is common to humanity. But God is faithful; he will not allow you to be tempted beyond what you are able, but with the temptation he will also provide the way out so that you may be able to bear it.

Imagine this: You're trapped in a maze, and everything looks the same—there are no distinguishing marks no matter where you go. With every turn, you become more panicked. Then, you make a turn and you see a faint glimmer of light. As you get closer to the light, you can clearly see how to escape the maze. At that point, would you turn around and look for another way to get out, or would you take the path before you?

As long as you are alive, you will face temptation; but God loves you. As Paul said, God will always provide a way out from temptation. Our job is to take the way out that He provides.

When Satan tempted Job, God gave Satan parameters which he had to abide by. He does the same on your behalf. The words "except what is common to humanity" show that you aren't tempted in any unique way from anyone else. These are God's words, and He promised to always give you a way out of temptation. It's up to you to rely on the Holy Spirit and practice self-control to follow the light to the exit each time.

delight |

How have you experienced God's faithfulness when you've been tempted?

Why is it important to understand that all people face the same kinds of temptations?

display |

It's often difficult to resist temptation. However, when you are weak, God is strong (2 Cor. 12:9-10). He provides the way out, and He bears the weight so that you can handle the strain of it. You just have to declare your dependence on Him and follow as He leads you out.

Look around your house and find a flashlight. Throw it in your book bag or purse. Every time you see it click it on and off. Let it serve as a reminder that God's Word lights your path (Ps. 119:105). His Word will help you find the way out from temptation.

What you're facing might be more than you can handle, but that wasn't God's promise here. He promised you'd never face anything that He couldn't handle. Consider your life, and in a journal, write a poem or prayer asking God to handle a difficult situation for you.

Proclaim to God your belief in this verse and declare your dependence on Him. Express your appreciation for the escape plan He offers, and commit to Him that you will follow the way out that He provides.

day 17

WEAKNESS > STRENGTH

discover |

> Humbly admit to God that you're weak. Then, ask Him to take your weaknesses and turn them around to use them for His glory.

READ 2 CORINTHIANS 12:6-10.

But he said to me, "My grace is sufficient for you, for my power is perfected in weakness." Therefore, I will most gladly boast all the more about my weaknesses, so that Christ's power may reside in me. — 2 Corinthians 12:9

In a famous Old Testament battle, God whittled down the size of Israel's army from 22,000 to 300. He took away their traditional weapons and told them to blow horns, shatter pitchers, and raise torches (Judg. 7). He did this so that Israel would not, "elevate themselves over me and say, 'I saved myself'" (Judg. 7:2b). He actually made the army weaker so that His strength would shine through as He made them victorious.

God specializes in using the weak to accomplish things beyond their strength. This brings glory to God instead of us—He just worked through us to accomplish His plan (2 Cor. 4:7). The apostle Paul knew this all too well. So that he would continually rely on God's grace and strength, Paul was given what he called a "thorn in the flesh" (v. 7). God wasn't making things difficult for Paul; rather, this was God's way of showing Paul how much He could do through Paul if he relied on God's strength rather than his own. The same is true for us!

delight |

What was Paul's response to the "torment" he experienced?

Do you think you would respond the same way? Why or why not?

How have you seen God's power perfected in your weakness throughout your life?

How does God's promise to Paul soothe your heart when you're experiencing difficult days?

display |

Scripture is clear: even a person with extraordinary willpower is weak in comparison to God. When He makes us painfully aware of our weakness, it's just an opportunity to rely more on His strength.

List three weaknesses you struggle with often. Beside each one, write a way God can bring Himself glory and reveal His extraordinary strength through your weakness.

day 18

TREASURED WORD

discover|

Talk to God about your appreciation for His Word. Confess if you have not treasured it as you should. Ask God for new ways to take in more of His Word and become better equipped to face temptation through it.

READ PSALM 119:11.

I have treasured your word in my heart so that I may not sin against you.

Gummy vitamins are good for you and surprisingly delicious, but they aren't enough to sustain your life. You also need food, water, rest, and so on, or you will die. These devotions are like vitamins. Through them you can focus specifically on a few verses at a time and apply them. But spending a few minutes a day in this book is not enough to keep you alive spiritually. You must also spend time in prayer, worshiping and being taught the truths of God's Word.

Jesus—the embodiment of the Word (John 1:1)—knew how to perfectly use Scripture to combat temptation. As we grow in our spiritual life and learn more Scripture, we are better equipped to fight temptation and grow in self-control. So, for every way we take in Scripture, we have to make sure it sinks into our hearts. Treasure it soul-deep, and the Spirit will remind you of it when temptation arises. Look at the direct connection between treasuring God's Word and victory over sin in this verse. If we want to fight against sin, then we need to treasure Scripture.

delight |

To treasure something is to value it greatly. What do you treasure? How do people know you treasure it?

What is the difference between simply memorizing Scripture and treasuring God's Word in your heart? Explain.

display |

Wherever you are in your faith and Bible study journey, go beyond the verses on these pages as you study Scripture this month. Here are some tips to help you get started:

- Be sure that your study of Scripture is not simply to increase your academic knowledge of the Bible. Instead, view Scripture as a treasure. It is the ultimate source of truth, so hiding more of it in your heart better equips you to fight temptation and grow in self-control.

- With permission, listen to the Bible on audio through an app or device while traveling to and from school or other activities.

- Write out any Scripture you plan to memorize, then, under the verse, write out how this verse or passage affects you. For example, under today's verse, you might write: "I will treasure this verse because it is God's Word and teaches me to be self-controlled." You'll see that you have so many reasons to treasure God's Word!

- If you don't know where to begin, the Gospel of John is an excellent starting point. This Gospel was originally written to convince Gentiles that Jesus is God, and it shares the same message with us today!

day 19

ON THE INSIDE

discover|

READ 2 TIMOTHY 1:7.

God has not given us a spirit of fear, but one of power, love, and sound judgment.

Have you ever had to navigate your house with the lights off? As long as there are no unexpected obstacles on the floor, then you can probably do it without fear or hesitation. Why? Because you know what's on the inside of your house. As we go through life, we have the power to trust God's goodness instead of being fearful of what's around the corner. Rather than a spirit of fear, God has given us power, love, and sound judgment.

We know that His love will never leave us or abandon us, so we don't have to fear being alone (Deut. 31:6). Instead of being overwhelmed, with our heart racing over just the thought of temptation, we can remember that God's Spirit has given us sound judgment so we can resist. We can trust these gifts from Him, so we can navigate life—even the unexpected obstacles—with His power, love, and sound judgment.

> **Pray this verse today. Trade your fear for His power. Trade your fear for love because God's perfect love casts out all fear (1 John 4:18). Let go of your fear of rejection and trust that God gives you sound judgment.**

delight |

God has not given us a spirit of fear, so where does fear originate? Explain.

How are courage, power, love, and sound judgment helpful to living godly, self-controlled lives?

What do you think it means to have a "spirit of" a specific quality? What would it mean to have a spirit of self-control?

display |

This verse was originally written by the apostle Paul to a young pastor named Timothy. Maybe you can identify with these words. What challenging circumstances have you faced and had to choose God's power, love, and sound judgment over fear? Draw a symbol placing the words power, love, and sound judgment above fear to remind you that God has empowered you to live a self-controlled life through the Holy Spirit. Get as creative as you want!

List two scenarios in which you might lean toward fear, then reflect on the truth of this verse. Write out how God's power, love, and sound judgment might help you overcome that fear.

God's Power is Greater Than Willpower

day 20

WEAK SPOTS

discover |

> Talk honestly and openly with God about what you desire.
> Be upfront about the things you want to do that honor Him.
> Then talk to Him about the evil desires that still live within
> you that you need Him to help you overcome.

READ JAMES 1:12-18.

*No one undergoing a trial should say, "I am being tempted by God," since God
is not tempted by evil, and he himself doesn't tempt anyone. But each person is
tempted when he is drawn away and enticed by his own evil desire.*
— James 1:13–14

Think about the next test in your most difficult class. Imagine that
as you begin taking the test, you find it to be more challenging
than you thought it would be. Suddenly, you remember the girl
next to you is the smartest person in the class. If you tilt your head
just right, then you can see directly onto her page. But is your
desire to cheat your teacher's fault? Of course not!

This scenario helps us understand today's Scripture. Yes, sometimes
God allows our faith to be tested, but He never tempts us to sin.
We are tempted by the sin nature we were born with combined
with our own desires. We have to know our weak spots. We have to
be aware of situations that might tempt us and rely on His Spirit to
show us the way out when temptation is unavoidable (See Day 16).

delight |

What words in these verses reveal who is exempt from temptation? Explain.

Highlight the words "drawn away" (v. 14). Look at the context of these words. How can you avoid being "drawn away"?

display |

It's important to know our weak spots and to recognize temptation for what it is when we see it. The truth is that everyone has been born with the natural desire to sin, and we will be fighting against it until the day we die. You are an eternal soul inside an imperfect body, where the perfect Holy Spirit dwells.

When you achieve victory over temptation through the Spirit, you take a step forward in your pursuit of holiness. Write out three instances where you experienced victory over temptation. Then, beside each one, write out how this will encourage you and help you have victory in the future.

On Day 14, you were encouraged to find an accountability partner. If you don't have an accountability partner yet, pray that God would connect you with someone you can share your life with and walk together with in faithfulness to God. If you have established accountability with a girl in your life who is also growing in Christ, then check in with her and ask how you can pray for her.

Respond or React

The truth of the matter is, people will do and say things that irritate, hurt, or upset us. But we can choose what we will do when this inevitably happens: We can choose to react or respond. To react usually means to act in opposition or against someone. To respond means to give an answer. Here's a simple way to distinguish between reacting and responding: a reaction is an impulse, gut-level action or reply, while a response is made after taking time to think through what has been said and giving a careful reply.[1]

Scripture cautions us to be slow to respond to hurtful words and actions: "Everyone should be quick to listen, slow to speak, and slow to anger" (Jas. 1:19). How can we do this right in the middle of a difficult situation? Let's take a look at a three-step process to help us.

Be quick to Listen. Learn to listen for what someone says and what she doesn't say. Watch body language, facial expressions, and listen to tone of voice. For example, crossed arms could indicate defensiveness or tapping fingers could mean impatience. Eye contact and standing up straight usually point to confidence, while smiling to the point where the eyes crinkle makes people appear warm and welcoming.[2] The volume, speed, and even breathiness with which we speak also communicates something about our underlying feelings.

If we're quick to listen, we'll take a step back and look at the bigger picture. We'll wonder what's going on in that person's life in this moment and outside of it. Look at everything before you look at this one thing. As you're paying attention to tone, body language, and facial cues, it is still important to listen to the words someone says. Do they repeat words, or is there a common theme? Listen attentively.

Then, take a deep breath before you respond. For one, this calms you and helps you to think clearer. Breathing deeply also creates space to remember that God cares about the pain you're feeling in that moment and the pain the one who hurt you may be feeling as well. So, give your cares over to Him (1 Pet. 5:7).

Be slow to speak. This means letting what you've heard sink in before you respond. Before you try to figure out how what she said relates to you, continue on with your listening skills to make sure you've understood. Here, it can be a good idea to summarize aloud for her what you understood her to say. Then, check for understanding with a statement like, "I want to make sure I understand. Is this what you meant?" Give your friend a chance to respond, then summarize and clarify again before moving forward. This ensures that you truly understand what it is you're responding to and that allows the other girl to feel like you value her thoughts, feelings, and words.

Now, take a beat to ask yourself if what your friend is saying is accurate. If it is, apologize. Then, ask God to help you change your response in the future. It can also be helpful to ask something like: "How can I word things differently in the future? I want to speak the truth in a way that's helpful to you rather than harmful." If not, think about this person. What's her character like? What's going on in her life outside of work? How might that be causing her to speak to you? Then, consider saying something like, "It sounds like you're having a rough morning. What can I do to help?" Sometimes, all others need to know is that someone cares and is there to listen and help.

Be slow to anger. You'll notice that all three of these actions—even if they are an active waiting—connect and build on one another. Part of being slow to anger is continuing to consider the bigger picture. But here, we want to focus on the biggest picture. Rather than only looking at what's going on in that person's life, we want to look to what God says to do. We look to His character and His plan to guide our responses. Here are three key things to remember:

- Every person, regardless of how she treats you, is made in the image of God.
- God has the ultimate say: He is the one who gets to decide when and what consequences people will receive when they treat others poorly.
- God calls us to love others as He has loved us—basically, we love no matter what (John 13:34; 1 John 4:19).

If a girl is unkind or hurtful to you out of spite, you are still called to respond in love and kindness. Now, this doesn't mean being a doormat. You can kindly set boundaries for how you will or won't be treated and clearly communicate those. This is a loving action both for yourself and others. However, at the end of the day, you belong to God and everything you say and do reflects on Him. When someone hurts you and you haven't sinned against her (or have apologized for sinning against her), then remember that the situation rests securely in God's hands. What better place could it be? Ultimately, God is the one who will set all things right (Rom. 12:19).

My Story

Take a minute to write about a difficult situation you're experiencing. In a journal, write out how you can engage with that girl (or those girls) by using the three-step process outline in James 1:19. Then pray that God would give you the strength and wisdom to carry it out.

day 21

MEASURE TWICE, CUT ONCE

discover

> Ask God to prepare your heart to receive a difficult truth from His Word today. Ask for His help in seeing yourself accurately. Commit to listen to what the Spirit shows you about your anger, speech, and ability to listen.

READ JAMES 1:19-21.

My dear brothers and sisters, understand this: Everyone should be quick to listen, slow to speak, and slow to anger, or human anger does not accomplish God's righteousness. — James 1:19-20

If you've ever made cookies from scratch, then you know how important it is to measure flour carefully. The amount of flour must be exact or the cookies will be too fluffy or too flat. Once the flour is added to the recipe, it's almost impossible to remove! Moving slowly and measuring carefully through the process helps you accomplish what you set out to achieve—making a delicious cookie.

This illustrates James' process for walking in righteousness. It all starts with listening well. Speaking too quickly indicates that we probably haven't given our full attention to the girl who's talking. If we first listen well, then measure our words carefully, we're less likely to become angry. When we're absolutely fuming, we aren't able to accomplish God's righteousness in that moment. Just like you measure carefully in baking, measure your words carefully too.

delight |

Why is human anger incompatible with God's righteousness?

List three people who are "quick to listen" and describe how you feel about each of them.

display |

One of the keys to being quick to listen, slow to speak, and slow to anger is to have a teachable spirit. When we feel like we know it all or are always right, we'll be less likely to listen. We'll feel like we have the answers and others should listen to what we have to say. Then if they don't listen to us, we'll probably get angry. It's a vicious cycle!

Pay attention to the words you speak today. Consider taking a small note book or note card with you wherever you go. Whenever you catch yourself speaking negatively to or about someone or using corrective phrases like "Actually..." and "But listen to me..."—write them down. Tomorrow, under each phrase, make a tally for each time you were able to stop yourself from inserting your opinion—even if you believed you were right.

But, there might be moments when you do need to share a correct understanding about someone or something (especially if it's a spiritual matter). If that happens, season your words with grace (Col. 4:6) so that you might be heard rather than dismissed as a know it all. Consider one of the issues you encountered yesterday. Do any truly need to be corrected? Write out a simple way you could offer gentle, gracious correction when the opportunity arises.

day 22

THE WRONG QUESTION

discover|

READ 1 THESSALONIANS 4:3-8.

For this is God's will, your sanctification: that you keep away from sexual immorality, that each of you knows how to control his own body in holiness and honor, not with lustful passions, like the Gentiles, who don't know God.
— 1 Thessalonians 4:3-5

"How far is too far?" This classic question people ask when it comes to dating is the wrong question. We generally want to hear that there is a clear line where everything less is okay and everything beyond is not. Here's the bottom line: There is a time and a place for physical intimacy—and that place is marriage. Yes, the standard is high, but we are called to the highest standard of holiness.

To be sanctified is to be set apart. This passage clearly states one aspect of God's will for your life and future: your sanctification (v. 3). The process of sanctification applies to every part of your existence. These verses describe what the sanctified person looks like. Is your online activity holy and honorable? Is your every physical interaction with your boyfriend holy and honorable? Those who worshiped false gods in Paul's day did not have the convicting presence of the Holy Spirit that you have. So, control your own body and make drastic sacrifices to avoid sexual immorality not sneak closer to it.

delight |

How does avoiding sexual immorality lead to sanctification?

It is your responsibility to learn to control your own body, but you are not alone in this pursuit. How does God help you learn to do this?

display |

The reason the classic question is the wrong question is because it looks in the wrong direction, asking, "How close can I get to sin?" The better question and view is, "How close can I get to holiness?" If an action leads toward sexual immorality rather than away from it, get rid of it. Self-control is a matter of holiness. So, draw toward holiness rather than away from it. In a journal, list a few areas where you're tempted to get close to sin. Then, beside each one, write down how you can turn toward holiness instead.

On an index card, write out the words: *I can honor God with my body when I pursue holiness instead of sin*. Keep the card with you. Whenever you're tempted to inch closer to sin, take out the card and read it as a reminder to pursue God instead.

If you struggle with looking at images or videos that don't honor God or other people, then limit your use of technology. Talk with your parents or guardians—no matter how uncomfortable that might seem—and ask about an app or service that filters out any inappropriate content from your devices.

> Ask God to help you seek His will above all in your life. Pray that you would truly understand that and live like His holiness matters more than momentary pleasure. Ask Him to help you remember His grace is sufficient—no matter what.

day 23

MAKE THE MOST OF IT!

discover

> Talk to God about where you stand on alcohol before you are of the legal age to drink. Resolve to show self-control in this area. If you have stumbled with drugs or alcohol, confess it to God and rest in the grace He gives you.

READ EPHESIANS 5:15-21.

Pay careful attention, then, to how you walk—not as unwise people but as wise—making the most of the time, because the days are evil. So don't be foolish, but understand what the Lord's will is. And don't get drunk with wine, which leads to reckless living, but be filled by the Spirit. — Ephesians 5:15-18

Do you know that palms-sweating, anxious, excited feeling of watching the end of a close game, race, or debate? The final moments are vital to the outcome! So, when the participants don't give all they have, the fans can be a little, well, passionate. These close calls can be pretty exciting!

Today's Scripture explored this same idea, but from a spiritual perspective. Hopefully, you'll live for years to come, but you don't know for sure how much time you have left. The apostle Paul encouraged the Ephesians to acknowledge this uncertainty and embrace their time on earth, making the most of it. As a result of the Holy Spirit's presence in your life and the unknown number of days you have left, you should do the same. This means it is unwise to waste your days abusing substances like drugs and alcohol.

delight |

How does abusing drugs and alcohol lead to reckless living?

How does choosing to be filled with the Holy Spirit help you avoid the recklessness brought on by substance abuse?

display |

The way we live as Christ followers should be noticeably different than those who don't know Him. We have a higher calling on our lives than drunkenness and drugs. We are called to control what we consume too.

Paul said understanding God's will helps us make the most of our time and being filled by the Spirit helps us avoid "reckless living" (v. 18).

- Write out anything that you know is God's will for His people, and jot down the Scripture reference beside it.

- Search on a Bible reference website or Bible app for the phrases "filled by the Spirit" and "filled with the Spirit." Choose two verses that help you understand this idea better and journal about how they will influence you as you pursue holiness.

Write out a quick rundown of your daily schedule in a planner or journal. Pray over it and ask God to help you make the most of the day. If you are tempted to abuse drugs or alcohol, think about how that would cost you the productivity of the day, both personally and for the kingdom of God.

day 24

SPEAKING LIFE

discover|

READ EPHESIANS 4:25-31.

Therefore, putting away lying, speak the truth, each one to his neighbor, because we are members of one another. Be angry and do not sin. Don't let the sun go down on your anger, and don't give the devil an opportunity.
— Ephesians 4:25-27

We've seen that self-control is demonstrated in our bodily conduct, but what about the way we talk to people? Through our words we share the message of the gospel, and the Holy Spirit changes people's hearts. Honoring God with our whole selves means exercising self-control in our speech too.

> Confess to God any lies you have told, and set the record straight if possible. Pray for the strength to make peace with others as you can. Ask God to use your speech for good.

In three different verses in today's passage, Paul laid out areas of speech that the Ephesians needed to bring under the lordship of Christ. These included lying—intentionally deceiving others with words (v. 26); foul language and tearing others down (v. 29); and shouting and slandering others with words (v. 31). Though different, each of these sins is carried out through speech. With our words, we have the opportunity to speak grace into peoples lives; to be a blessing and not a curse. Words can bring hope or destruction; they can even lead to eternal life or death. We just have to decide how we will let the Lord use our words.

delight |

Why is it important to God that Christians not lie to one another?

Consider when you're most tempted to gossip, use foul language, or shout. How could the enemy tempt you into sinful speech in these areas?

display |

Spirit-filled Christians do not gossip, say mean things to get revenge or to get back at others with their words. It's confusing for people to hear profanity and songs of praise come from the same lips.

Think of one of the areas of temptation you listed. Choose a Bible verse that speaks to that issue. Memorize it. Anytime you're tempted to speak in an unholy way, say the verse to yourself—or say it aloud if you need to! Be prepared with words that point to God and His goodness.

What words did you use today? Write them out. Draw a red X through any that were negative or harmful to others, and commit to eliminating them from your vocabulary. Then, replace them with encouraging words to others. Trade bitterness for grace, and watch as people respond to the positivity, hope, and encouragement you bring to their lives through your words.

day 25

ONLINE LEGACY

discover

> Even if you're not on social media, ask God to continue to shape the way you speak to people. Ask Him to take over your words so that they give life to others.

READ COLOSSIANS 4:5-6.

Act wisely toward outsiders, making the most of the time. Let your speech always be gracious, seasoned with salt, so that you may know how you should answer each person.

If someone pulled up your social media feed ten years from now, what would they find? What would the think about you at that age? We have a written and pictorial online legacy, so consider what legacy you might be making and what it says about your relationship with Christ.

Gracious words on social media are like delicious food. We must be wise in our interactions toward those outside the Christian faith (v. 5), including our online interactions. When our online words are not gracious, it reflects not just on us but on our church, our brothers and sisters in Christ, and even on Jesus Himself. Along with the occasional funny cat video, what better purpose could there be for your online platform than to help others know and see the goodness of God? Practicing godly self-control includes your words on social media.

delight |

List three ways you can use your online presence to glorify God and help others know Christ.

In verse 6, Paul encourages us to know how to respond to each person. Why might it be important to know how to give truthful answers compassionately before the situation ever arises?

How might paying attention to others help you respond to them graciously?

display |

In Matthew 28:18-20, Jesus gave us the Great Commission, sending us out to make disciples of all nations. This is why we are called to act wisely toward those who do not yet believe in Jesus. A foolish social media post or reply in a comment thread can turn someone off to the gospel. Sharing things that are untrue robs us of credibility. Making our profiles into shrines about how awesome we are worships self instead of God. Blatant use of profanity sends a mixed message when we also proclaim Christ. Instead, our social media presence should always be gracious (v. 6).

People who learn that you stand for the gospel may search your profile to see if you're the real deal. The good news is that you have the ability, and even the obligation, to remove past posts that no longer line up with your convictions. Delete any social media posts that don't bring honor to God. Share John 3:16 online. Let any discussion you have as a result of the post be seasoned with grace.

day 26

COVERED IN DUST

discover |

Ask God to help you see all that you have as His, especially money. Submit your financial resources, great or small, to the lordship of Christ.

READ MATTHEW 6:19-24.

"Store up for yourselves treasures in heaven, where neither moth nor rust destroys, and where thieves don't break in and steal. For where your treasure is, there your heart will be also." — Matthew 6:20–21

There are dust-covered things in our attics or garages right now that we once cherished. Plenty of online platforms are packed with junk for sale by people who once had to have these things; people who stood in line for hours to be the first to have phones that are now obsolete. Stuff, no matter how expensive or in demand it might be, will one day all be worthless and go away.

What we do with our money and stuff indicates what is happening in our hearts. Scripture makes it clear: "You cannot serve both God and money" (v. 24). People can end up worshiping money and stuff, banking their lives on things that don't last forever, while going bankrupt with their souls that will live for eternity. We are all tempted to give a higher priority to money and our physical belongings, but these things must be mastered in self-control too.

delight |

What is something that you once wanted so badly but now is collecting dust somewhere? How does this help you understand today's Scripture?

How do you store up for yourself treasure in heaven?

display |

Check your heart for bad spending habits. If you are prone to chasing the latest fad that will soon go out of style and be discarded, pray honestly about what that says about your heart and its desire for the things of this world.

List the last three items you desperately wanted. Beside each item, write ways it can bring glory to God. If it is something that leads you away from God, think about ways that you can reverse that trend.

Think about that one thing you desperately want right now. Is it something that will be collecting dust in a matter of time? Is it something that leads you away from God? If not, consider how you might use the money you would have spent on that item to glorify God.

My dear brothers and sisters, understand this: Everyone should be quick to listen, slow to speak, and slow to anger, for human anger does not accomplish God's righteousness.

JAMES 1:19-20

day 27

HIS TEMPLE

discover|

> Ask God to prepare your heart to hear a tough truth today.
> Proclaim to God your trust in His love for you as His child.
> Tell Him that He is Lord over every aspect of your life.
> Then, follow the Holy Spirit where He takes you with this
> Scripture—even if it is painful at first.

READ PROVERBS 23:19-21.

For the drunkard and the glutton will become poor, and grogginess will clothe
them in rags. — Proverbs 23:21

We have to practice self-control in all areas of our lives. We can't
pick and choose what we allow God to bring under self-control in
and what we don't. Today, the Scripture mentioned two areas, one
of which many of us struggle to bring under self-control.

These two areas are alcohol (covered on Day 23) and gluttony.
Gluttony, or overeating, is something that often gets swept under
the rug. There are a variety of reasons why people overeat, ranging
from the emotional to a lack of nutritional understanding. The point
is not to shame anyone for what they eat, but to make clear that
what and how much we eat matters.

Our bodies are a temple of the Lord, so we shouldn't misuse our
bodies (1 Cor. 6:19-20). Gluttony misuses our bodies. If our bodies
are unhealthy, we are not as useful to the Lord as we could be. So
we must treat our bodies right, by eating healthy and exercising.

---

delight |

Why is it helpful to consider where our behaviors ultimately take us?

What effects can chronic overeating have on your future?

display |

The Bible says not to even associate with people "who drink too much wine or with those who gorge themselves on meat" (v. 20). Look around your life. Are you being influenced in unhealthy ways? List two steps you can take now to pursue healthier influences—spiritually, mentally, emotionally, and physically.

Look at yourself in the mirror. When you do, see a beloved child of God above all else. Then, look honestly and see if there are opportunities to grow in self-control. Look honestly at the straight line that connects your choices to your physical well being. The great news is that self-control comes from the Holy Spirit. This is a spiritual matter and, as God's beloved child, you are not alone in this. You are His. On day 15 you were challenged to write on an index card, *I am His*. Find that card again and underline the phrase written there. Keep that card close as a reminder that you are His beloved child, special and wonderful. Let it encourage you toward self-control in all areas of life.

Please know, if you struggle with an eating disorder, you are so loved, beautiful, and incredibly valued by God. Please consider reaching out to a parent, guardian, youth pastor, small group leader—a godly adult you can trust—if you're struggling. They can support you and point you toward helpful resources.

day 28

DON'T RUIN THE PAINT

discover

The mindset of the flesh is hostile to God because it does not submit to God's law. Indeed, it is unable to do so. Those who are in the flesh cannot please God. You, however, are not in the flesh, but in the Spirit, if indeed the Spirit of God lives in you. If anyone does not have the Spirit of Christ, he does not belong to him.

Consider this scenario: You're in art class. You want pink paint, but the pink paint is out, so the only way to make that happen is to mix the red and the white. You squirt the white paint onto the pallet, then you pick up the bottle of red. You add and stir until you have the perfect shade of pink. But when you got up to grab a brush, the girl next to you accidentally flung a big drop of lime green into your paint! No matter how small the amount of green paint, your mixture is ruined.

Apply this idea to sin: There is no such thing as a little bit of sin. Mixing a little bit of sin in our lives is like adding a big drop of green to pink paint and expecting pink. If we want to walk with the Holy Spirit, we have to be all-in. "Just" a drop of sin that we tolerate could ruin what He wants to do in your life. Repentance means turning away from sin. We can't let just a little bit of our former lives—which were hostile to God—remain in our hearts. The Holy Spirit and even a little sin do not mix. God does not compromise, so we shouldn't either.

delight |

What about the flesh makes it hostile to God (v. 7)?

What do these verses tell us about people who have absolutely zero conviction for sin, no repentance, and no fruit of the Spirit in their lives?

display |

While we can't look into another girl's heart and know if she is in Christ or not, we can look at the fruit of her life. If a girl has no conviction for her sins and bears no fruit of the Spirit's activity in her life, then it is safe to assume she doesn't know Jesus. Jesus changes a person. He completely changes her way of life.

If you wonder about your salvation because you still have a drop of sin in your life, don't doubt. Repent and ask God to help you turn away from it. The desire not to sin—much clearer than the sin you may still struggle with—reveals the true condition of your heart. You will never be perfect, but if the driving force of your life is to pursue holiness and be like Christ, then you are on track. Rest in that truth. Design a lock-screen with the word *rest* to remind you.

Confess whatever "drop" of sin is in your life. Adapt the opening words of verse 9 into a prayer: "I am not in the flesh, but in the Spirit."

day 29

DOG EAT DOG

discover |

READ GALATIANS 5:13-15.

For you were called to be free, brothers and sisters; only don't use this freedom as an opportunity for the flesh, but serve one another through love. For the whole law is fulfilled in one statement: Love your neighbor as yourself. But if you bite and devour one another, watch out, or you will be consumed by one another.

Have you ever heard the phrase, "It's a dog eat dog world"? This phrase is a way to describe a viciously competitive environment. Maybe you've experienced this trying to make a team, or advance a chair in band, or compete for a scholarship. People who will stop at nothing to get what they want are dangerous. Today's Scripture warns of this behavior. If you will do anything to get what you want, someone else is usually willing to do more. In this arrangement both end up consuming each other.

Some of Paul's original readers were infected with the idea that Christians needed both Jesus and strict adherence to the Old Testament law to be saved. The reality is that Jesus alone saves us. As they argued, Christians were tearing one another down instead of serving one another in love like Jesus calls His followers to do. The freedom we are called to is not to abuse others, but to serve one another in love. We must bring under self-control the desire to get into that dog eat dog situation, which only leaves ruin in its wake.

delight |

How can you keep from being consumed by the "dog eat dog" situations you might experience in life?

What would the ultimate outcome be for this church if they continued tearing apart one another over this issue (v. 15)?

> **Lift your pastor and leaders up in prayer. Pray for unity in your church.**

display |

In Galatians 5:16-26, Paul described the stark differences between the outcomes of a mindset driven by the flesh and a mindset driven by the Spirit. Love for one another, especially in the church, is both an outcome of the Spirit's presence and a perfect fulfillment of what Jesus established when He proclaimed the Law fulfilled by our love for God and for one another (John 13:35).

If your church is experiencing conflict right now, take a note from one of the first churches of the New Testament and let love and grace win.

If you have lingering tension with someone in your church, then own every bit of it that is your fault according to the Bible and make things right. Even if there is no conflict in your life or church, increase your love. By the gifts the Spirit has given you, serve just like this text instructs. Be an active contributor in your church's mission to reach your community and watch the bond of love increase.

day 30

FRESH & CLEAN

discover |

READ 1 JOHN 1:9.

If we confess our sins, he is faithful and righteous to forgive us our sins and to cleanse us from all unrighteousness.

Do you remember the colossal messes you made and how unbelievably dirty you would get as a child? Unless you have the irremovable chocolate stain on your face from ten years ago, there has never been a mess that a shower could not clean. A nice, hot shower after a long day can make you feel like a new person! This feeling parallels a spiritual truth. There is never a stain on our souls that God's inexhaustible grace cannot completely wash away.

This unending renewal comes from God's faithfulness to us, not our faithfulness to Him. It flows from His righteousness, which will not be emptied even though it forgives countless Christians every minute of every day. The word "all" here is important. Yes, God has forgiven you even for that sin for which you have not yet forgiven yourself. The Bible says "all," and that means *all*.

As you have worked through this devotional, you may have felt some discouragement when you came to an area where you struggle to have self-control. Don't be discouraged. Confess it to God and ask Him to help you. He will—He loves to show us grace and forgiveness! It is not His desire for you to abuse His grace and forgiveness, but to let what He freely gives change your heart and make you more like Jesus in the process.

delight |

What is the difference between receiving God's grace for your sin and abusing God's grace for your sin?

Describe what it feels like to be cleansed by the faithfulness and righteousness of God.

display |

God is omniscient. Confessing sin to Him doesn't tell Him something He didn't already know. Instead, it brings back the honesty to your relationship with Him. Your forgiveness was secured by Christ's crucifixion and resurrection. So, without mistaking His grace for permission to sin, take full advantage of the grace purchased by Jesus on the cross and confess every time you sin. Do not repeatedly beat yourself up for sin, but believe this verse instead. "As far as the east is from the west, so far has he removed our transgressions from us" (Ps. 103:12).

When you fail at self-control in the future, ask God to forgive you and cleanse you from unrighteousness right away. Give yourself a physical reminder of this verse. Grab a bar of soap, put it in a sandwich bag, and throw it in your purse or backpack. As you smell the soap throughout the day, let it remind you of that fresh and clean feeling you get after a shower, which reflects the forgiveness God offers us through His grace.

Tell God that you believe He is faithful and righteous. Because you believe this and trust Him, confess your sin to Him. Feel the forgiveness. Smile because you are cleansed and made new in His love.

God's Power is Greater Than Willpower

When to Say Yes and When to Say No

People have an innate desire to be needed. While the roots of this behavior aren't necessarily negative, they can grow into a monstrous desire to say yes to everything. When it remains at a healthy level, our need to be needed plays a vital role in building healthy community—something we are called to do as believers. However, at an unhealthy level, this need to be needed and loved, to serve, to give—all in exchange for love—can become consuming, even to the point of becoming our identity. "After all," we might think, "if I'm not needed, then who am I?"

We have to exercise extreme caution here. Throughout the Bible, people are called to be meek and humble and to put others needs above our own. The beatitudes say those who are humble are blessed and "will inherit the earth" (v. 5). Peter says women should be adorned by "the hidden person of the heart with the imperishable beauty of a gentle and quiet spirit, which in God's sight is very precious" (1 Pet. 3:4). And Proverbs 31 is filled with descriptions that can seem impossible to live up to! This woman:

- is trustworthy,
- rises before dawn to provide food for her household,
- buys and sells goods,
- works hard and with a willing heart,
- is a savvy businesswoman,
- is physically strong,
- makes a profit in her earnings and she's always prepared,
- weaves clothes and other goods,
- gives to and serves the poor,
- builds up her husband and household,
- sells garments,
- is honorable and strong,
- laughs rather than worries,
- speaks wisdom and instructs with love,
- watches over her house,
- is never idle,
- is spoken of respectfully by her family,
- fears the Lord,
- receives rewards from Him for her obedience.

With a list like that, it's easy for us to feel like we have to fill our days to the brim and stress ourselves out to do every little thing. It's easy for us to believe we have to work hard and do everything right to gain the approval of God—and everyone else. But that isn't the case. The work we do is more about our motive for doing so. As Colossians 3:23-24 says: "Whatever you do, do it from the heart, as something done for the Lord and not for people, knowing that you will receive the reward of an inheritance from the Lord. You serve the Lord Christ."

So, when exactly does the need to be needed move past the biblical command to love and serve the Lord and others into an unhealthy obsession with giving of oneself in exchange for love? How do we guard against it?

We have to recognize a truth we've seen time and time again throughout this devotional: We must also exercise self-control. Think about all the times Jesus went away to be alone to pray. Think of how He took a nap in a boat, in the middle of a storm. Think of the command to the disciples to leave and "shake the dust off your feet" when people didn't want to hear their message of the gospel. If we want to do anything well, we have to set boundaries and have the self-control to keep them in place when we do.

It's also important to recognize that we don't say no to be mean or vindictive or selfish. We say no when it is necessary. We may even say no sometimes to good things so that we can say yes to even better things. We say no to open ourselves up to a better "yes," to the "yes" God wants from us.

The goal of self-control is not to be mastered by any of our desires—even a perpetual need to be needed. Instead, the goal is to follow Jesus' example of being in the world but not of the world, of when to say yes and when to say no. We are very much a part of this world, yet at the same time, we belong to God's kingdom. We have to learn to both live in it and lead it toward God and His love. We cannot do this without self-control, without learning balance and boundaries.

When faced with a new opportunity to serve, try asking yourself the following questions.

How does this fit within the gifts and resources God has given to me?

If it doesn't, what might God be trying to teach me by serving this way?

This opportunity will take a good bit of time, but I believe God is calling me to it. What can I let go of to create the appropriate space in my schedule to serve this way?

What do I need that I currently don't have to take this opportunity?

Where else might God be calling me to serve instead?

Why do I want to say yes? Do I truly believe it's for God's glory and the good of others? Or is it for my own recognition and so I can look good to others?

How can I respond in love and kindness when other people—even well-meaning believers—push me to serve in an area I don't believe God has called me to serve?

Who is a safe person who can hold me accountable to say yes only when it's clear that God wants me to say yes?

For further study, check out "The Best Yes," by Lysa TerKeurst

My Weakness, His Strengths

In the Day 20 Devo: *Weak Spots*, we learned that to avoid temptation requires us to know our weak spots. While it can be unhealthy to exclusively focus on our weaknesses and failures, it is actually healthy to acknowledge them and know them well enough to defend against them. Spend some time in prayer, asking the Holy Spirit to guide you as you examine your heart, determining areas of weakness in your life.

In the column labeled, "When I am Weak," write out any personal struggles that come to mind. Then, look to Scripture. Beside each "weakness," in the column labeled, "God is Strong," write out a Scripture that speaks specifically to that weakness or encourages you to be strong. The first is filled in for you as an example.

WHEN I AM WEAK	GOD IS STRONG
I am often tempted to gossip about my friends.	Instead of gossiping, God calls us to speak words that bring life and build up others (Eph 4:29).

Sources

1. Matthew B. James, "React vs Respond," Psychology Today (Sussex Publishers, September 1, 2016), https://www.psychologytoday.com/us/blog/focus-forgiveness/201609/react-vs-respond.
2. "22 Body Language Examples And What They Show," Betterhelp (BetterHelp, October 20, 2018), https://www.betterhelp.com/advice/body-language/22-body-language-examples-and-what-they-show/.